Teach Me
The Fear of the Lord

10 CHALLENGING LESSONS

by Lucius Malcolm

AKA Christian Publishing, LLC
964 Vera Court
Winder, GA 30680
470-773-8649;
info@akachristianpublishing.com

Copyright 2025. All rights reserved solely by the author.
ISBN: 979-8-9889696-7-9

The author guarantees all contents are original and do not infringe upon legal rights of any other person or work.
No part of this book may be reproduced in any form without the permission of the author.
Artwork inside the book was created by N. Malcolm.
Unless otherwise indicated, Scripture quotations are taken with permission from the New American Standard Bible (NASB).
Scripture taken from the NEW AMERICAN STANDARD BIBLE™, Copyright©1960,1962,1963,1968,1971,1972,1973, 1975,1977,1995 by The Lockman Foundation. Used by permission.
Scriptures marked KJV are taken from the KING JAMES VERSION (KJV): KING JAMES VERSION, public domain.
Scriptures marked ESV are taken from the THE HOLY BIBLE, ENGLISH STANDARD VERSION (ESV): Scriptures taken from THE HOLY BIBLE, ENGLISH STANDARD VERSION ® Copyright© 2001 by Crossway, a publishing ministry of Good News Publishers. Used by permission.

The content presented in this book is based on the author's perspective and interpretation of the subject matter. Neither the publisher nor any associated parties shall be held responsible for any consequences arising from the opinions or interpretations expressed with in this book.

The cover is the *Sacrifice of Isaac* by Rembrandt, 1635.
Hermitage Museum, St. Petersburg.
Public domain. Image via Wikimedia Commons.

"The importance of 'fearing God' is illustrated throughout the Bible, from Genesis to Revelation. Yet, despite its mention throughout scripture, it is likely that few Christians fully understand what it means to fear God. In 10 fascinating lessons, Lucius Malcolm dives deep into the subject, illustrating the importance of acknowledging God's majesty, the comfort of God's sovereignty, and the blessings that await those who truly fear the Lord. Certainly a study worth revisiting often."
— Dr. Karl V. Miller, Professor Emeritus

"This book is a must-read for followers of our Savior and Lord, Jesus Christ. It is a very rich, easy-to-read type of book that dissects profound truths from God's word. I believe the topic of the fear of the Lord is so critical to the believer's sanctification journey, yet it's not so often discussed. It is assumed that Christians automatically have a healthy fear of God, but this book delves into the specific areas that we may easily neglect. I strongly believe that the revelation from the numerous scriptures that admonish us to fear the Lord will have a positive and transformative impact on every reader's life. I am so delighted to endorse this book."
— Dr. Juliet Sekandi,
   Global Health Institute, Epidemiology & Biostatistics
   Associate Professor & Associate Director
   Graduate Coordinator, Certificate in Global Health

Foreword

When most people think "fear of the Lord," they misunderstand or are confused about the meaning. Many assume it means we are to be afraid of God. If one is not right with God through salvation in Jesus, then perhaps one should be afraid of God, but that is not what God desires. He created us for a relationship with Him. Our sin separates us from His holy presence, but the good news is that Jesus paid the penalty for our sin so that we could be forgiven and restored to a right relationship with Him.

Once we are saved and declared righteous by Christ's substitutionary work on the cross, we need to develop a healthy "fear of the Lord." This does not mean we are afraid of Him and keep our distance. Instead, it means we properly draw near to Him and stay close to Him through a reverential respect for His full nature. Did you get that last phrase? "Reverential respect for His full nature." This is one of the keys to the fear of the Lord–knowing His full nature. If we don't properly know who God is, then how can we properly respond to Him?

In this book, Lucius helps us to know God better so that we can properly respond to Him. The Word of God promises endless blessings to those who respond with a proper fear of the Lord. Allow the Holy Spirit to be your teacher as you go on this journey!

Dr. David Holt
Pastor of Living Hope Church
Athens, Georgia

Introduction

When we discuss or even mention "the fear of the Lord," most people avoid it or relegate it to the Old Testament or Old Covenant. However, Scripture emphasizes its importance over and over with such phrases as "the fear of the LORD is the beginning of knowledge," "the fear of the LORD is the beginning of wisdom," and "the fear of the LORD is the instruction for wisdom."

As these verses of truth began to sink into my mind and spirit, I became more and more interested in what "the fear of the Lord" really means. This caused me to ask this question: Should I ask God to teach me the fear of the Lord? The question itself brought hesitation and, yes, I must admit, a type of fear. So I wrestled with it for weeks, finally surrendering to the voice of the Spirit to indeed ask that very question.

The following lessons reveal the answer to that question.

– *Lucius Malcolm*

Note: In writing this, I have assumed that you are a mature, born-again Christian who is walking with Jesus and has a good understanding of His love for you. These lessons in no way replace or negate the love of God through Jesus Christ. Instead, they should deepen your understanding of that love and of the person of God.

Table of Contents

Lesson	Title	Page
1	"I Am Everything; You are Nothing"	9
2	"You Recognize My Lordship, My Kingship, and My Authority"	15
3	"You Wait Only Upon Me–Nothing and No One Else"	19
4	"You Give Up to Me Your Most Precious Possession"	25
5	"You Approach Me with a Broken and Contrite Heart"	29
6	"When You Truly Fear Me, You Need Not Fear Anything or Anyone Else"	35
7	"When You Truly Fear Me, It Brings the Highest Form of Revelation"	39
8	"When You Fear Me, a New Hope Arises in Your Soul, Knowing that the Victory is Certain"	45
9	"When You Fear Me, You Delight in My Word, and Blessings Follow"	49
10	"When You Fear Me, My Wisdom Begins"	55
	Conclusion	59

Lesson 1

"I Am Everything; You Are Nothing"

The book of Job is truly a very interesting and relevant story in the Bible that shows us what fearing the Lord means. "*Behold, the fear of the Lord, that is wisdom,*" is a powerful statement spoken to Job in Job 21:28. This statement also reflects Job's experience in wrestling with God about the reason for existence. All of us can identify in some way with Job in either the loss of possessions, the loss of health, the loss of children, the loss of a spouse, or the loss of our faith in God and who He is. I encourage you to read Job's entire story to get the full picture.

In context, after many days of suffering physically, mentally, and emotionally (probably more than any man has ever suffered), Job finally began to question God and why He had allowed these tragedies to happen. His questioning warranted a response from God, and the following exchange took place:

Then the Lord said to Job, "Will the faultfinder contend with the Almighty? Let him who reproves God answer it." Then Job answered the Lord and said, "Behold, I am insignificant; what can I reply to You? I lay my hand on my mouth." (Job 40:1-4)

> *Therefore I [Job] retract, and I repent in dust and ashes.*
> *(Job 42:6)*

These Scriptures show that when we are confronted with the reality of who God truly is and what He can do, our reaction should be fear and awe, which puts us on our faces before Him with nothing to say and nothing to offer. However, we must ask ourselves: how much are we truly like Job? When life turns upon us and rends our insides out, how do we respond? Are we then the faultfinder who contends with God?

I would have to say yes. As the natural, fleshly man described in Romans 8, we would also be shaking our fists at God and asking Him why. What is the difference between us and Job?

Unlike Job, we have the Holy Spirit. We have a new nature. We are the very righteousness of God, and we have the power from God to fall on our knees or on our face and say, "You are God, I am not. Do with me what you will. I will give thanks to you no matter what."

The Apostle Paul said it this way:

> *But whatever things were gain to me, those things I have counted as loss for the sake of Christ. More than that, I count all things to be loss in view of the surpassing value of knowing Christ Jesus my Lord, for whom I have suffered the loss of all things, and count them but rubbish so that I may gain Christ.*
> *(Philippians 3:7-8)*

Later in history, another very unusual story reflects the same concept of "I Am Everything; You Are Nothing." In Daniel 4, Nebuchadnezzar, the king of Babylon, had been warned about his arrogant god-complex by Daniel, one of four young men who were captured in Israel and taken to Babylon to be trained in the Babylonian culture for serving as Chaldeans, or wise men. Some scholars think these are the same wise men who brought Jesus Christ the gifts.

Then, Nebuchadnezzar had a frightening dream involving a tree, an angelic watcher, a stump, a mind changed to a mind of a beast, and seven periods of time (See Daniel 4). Later, the dream, along with Daniel's warnings to the king, became a reality.

Nebuchadnezzar, like many of us today in our materialistic culture, allowed his position, possessions, and power to overcome him and take him captive. He had essentially become his own god. Validation of his god-ship came from his own efforts, which had attained him a powerful position and immense physical wealth:

> *The king reflected and said, "Is this not Babylon the great, which I myself have built as a royal residence by the might of my power and for the glory of my majesty?" (Daniel 4:30)*

The moment Nebuchadnezzar declared his greatness, his nightmarish dream was realized: something snapped in his brain, and he became like a cow, eating grass, growing hair all over his body, and walking on all fours. This psychiatric disorder now has a name: insania zoanthropica. The disorder has been documented several times in modern day. It causes the mind to think it is an animal instead of a human being—in the case of Nebuchadnezzar, a cow.

After seven years of literally being put out to pasture, Nebuchadnezzar came to his senses, and Scripture says this:

> *But at the end of that period, I, Nebuchadnezzar, raised my eyes toward heaven, and my reason returned to me, and I blessed the Most High and praised and honored Him who lives forever; for His dominion is an everlasting dominion, and His kingdom endures from generation to generation. All the inhabitants of the earth are accounted as nothing, but He does according to His will in the host of heaven and among the inhabitants of earth; and no one can ward off His hand or say to Him, "What have You done?" (Daniel 4:34-35)*

Did you get that? "All the inhabitants of the earth are accounted as nothing, but He does according to His will."

The Gospel of Matthew further states that we only find our greatness in life when we lose it. Think about how Nebuchadnezzar had access to all the best his world could offer, but lost his life to a disease. Compare Nebuchadnezzar's story to what Jesus says in Matthew 16:25-26:

> For whoever wishes to save his life will lose it; but whoever loses his life for My sake will find it. For what will it profit a man if he gains the whole world and forfeits his soul? Or what will a man give in exchange for his soul?

In saying this, Jesus was trying to communicate to the disciples and to us that as long as we think that we are everything (as Nebuchadnezzar thought), gaining the world and being our own boss, we have actually lost everything. But when we lose our life in Him–when we know we are nothing and He is everything–then and only then do we gain real, eternal life, and we begin to understand the fear of the Lord.

Nebuchadnezzar and Job were very different men, yet they learned the same lesson: God is everything, and I am nothing. For Job, it took literally losing everything for him to come to that realization and truly fear the Lord. For Nebuchadnezzar, it took him being reduced to a cow, eating grass with no power or authority over anything or anybody before he truly feared the Lord. What about you? What will it take?

Check out the following poem, keeping in mind that Ozymandias is another name for Nebuchadnezzar.

> "Ozymandias" by Percy Bysshe Shelley (1792-1822):
> I met a traveler from an antique land
> Who said: "Two vast and trunkless legs of stone
> Stand in the desert... Near them, on the sand,
> Half sunk, a shattered visage lies, whose frown,
> And wrinkled lip, and sneer of cold command,
> Tell that its sculptor well those passions read
> Which yet survive, stamped on these lifeless things,
> The hand that mocked them, and the heart that fed:
> And on the pedestal, these words appear:

'My name is Ozymandias, king of kings:
Look on my works, ye Mighty, and despair!'
Nothing besides remains. Round the decay
Of that colossal wreck, boundless and bare
The lone and level sands stretch far away."

Applying this Lesson:

1. Do you ever say things like "this is mine," "look what I have done," or "what will they think"? If so, you may want to allow the Holy Spirit to do a deep dive and find out who or what is really "everything" in your life.

2. Would it help to practice daily losing your life in and for Jesus by speaking out loud words such as, "Lord, this day does not belong to me. What do You have for me to do today?" Or you might say, "Lord, this money does not belong to me. What would You like to do with it?"

3. What other Scriptures can you think of that might fit this lesson?

4. Who amongst your family or friends exalted themselves so much that they were "put out to pasture"? Maybe they lost their jobs, became alcoholic, became abusive, or totally lost their way. If so, you may need to break some curses and heal some old wounds. (I would recommend one of Neil T. Anderson's books such as *Victory Over the Darkness* or *The Bondage Breaker*.)

Lesson 2

"You Recognize My Lordship, My Kingship, and My Authority"

As I entered into this lesson, I was surprised because I thought that surrendering my will to God was part of my salvation experience. However, I quickly began to learn the difference between surrender and complete subservience to the King who rules over all. Some of this subservience has to do with the perspective of being subject to the King and, therefore, completely under His authority. The other part of this realization is that there is an ongoing learning curve as we mature in our faith and slowly begin to release all rights to our individual personhood. This happens when we see ourselves as "bondslaves"—that is, a slave who has been set free but remains, by choice, under the rule of his master. Paul uses this to describe himself several times:

> *"Paul, a bondslave"* in Romans 1:1,
> *"ourselves as your bondslaves"* in 2 Corinthians. 4:5,
> and *"bondslaves of God"* in Titus 1:1.

We own nothing, not even ourselves; we are possessions of the King, the Master.

In Psalm 2, we get a glimpse into the throne room of

God as He laughs and scoffs at the kings of the earth who are blatantly rebelling against Him and against His anointed:

> Why are the nations in an uproar; and the peoples devising a vain thing? The kings of the earth take their stand, and the rulers take counsel together against the Lord and against His Anointed, saying "Let us tear their fetters apart and cast away their cords from us!" He who sits in the heavens laughs. The Lord scoffs at them. Then He will speak to them in His anger and terrify them in His fury, saying, "But as for Me, I have installed My King upon Zion, My holy mountain." (Psalm 2:1-6)

As I read these words–"anger," "terrify," and "fury"–I began to weep. I then fell to my knees and hid my face in my hands. I do not know how long I remained in this state; I lost track of time. This, for me, was a life-changing experience as I felt the weight of these words and what they mean for the last days that we will soon face.

The word for anger literally means "short nose," that is, "patience has run out, and time has come [or is up]." Terrify is a verb meaning "dismayed" or "terrified" and is sometimes used when a "sudden threat conveys great fear." Fury is a masculine noun meaning "heat," "fierceness," and "anger." These words bring a new understanding of the character and emotions of God. Then, with the same truth and mercy He always demonstrates, He gives the rulers and kings the necessary response to His anger:

> Now, therefore, O kings, show discernment; take warning, O judges of the earth. Worship the Lord with reverence and rejoice with trembling. Do homage to the Son, that He not become angry, and you perish in the way, for His wrath may soon be kindled. How blessed are all who take refuge in Him! (Psalm 2:10-12)

Did you get that? There is rejoicing with trembling. How is that possible? This is not rejoicing as we think of the word.

The Hebrew word for rejoice is "guwl." The prime root means to "spin around" (under the influence of any violent motion). It is a type of worship that involves the fear of a king and his power, a spinning around of our circumstances so that we find ourselves trembling at his feet, knowing that this is the only place of true refuge and protection. This also means that as you and I find this place of "rejoicing with trembling," we will not have to endure the consequences of not recognizing and worshiping the King of Kings, found in verse 9:

> *You shall break them with a rod of iron, you shall shatter them like earthenware. (Psalm 2:9)*

As I took a breath and listened to the Holy Spirit, I was taken to another biblical passage where there was worship and the casting or spinning of something. It was in John's book of Revelation, chapter 4:

> *And the four living creatures, each one of them having six wings, are full of eyes around and within; and day and night they do not cease to say, "Holy, holy, holy is the Lord God, the Almighty, who was and who is and who is to come." And when the living creatures give glory and honor and thanks to Him who sits on the throne, to Him who lives forever and ever, the twenty-four elders will fall down before Him who sits on the throne, and will worship Him who lives forever and ever, and will cast their crowns before the throne, saying, "Worthy are You, our Lord and our God, to receive glory and honor and power; for You created all things, and because of Your will they existed, and were created." (Revelation 4:8-11)*

Please note what the elders are doing: they fall down and cast their crowns before the throne at the same time. Here, we have the same "rejoicing with trembling" as we had in Psalm 2. The elders fall down ("tremble"), then they twist ("spin") in order to throw their crowns before the throne of the Lord God, the Almighty, and worship Him. According to Strong's Concordance, the word for "cast" is "βάλλω bállō," a primary verb meaning to throw in various applications, more or less violent or intense: arise, cast (out), or thrust. In this state of "rejoicing with trembling," they realize that He alone is worthy to receive glory, honor, and power, and it is He alone who created all things and allowed them to exist.

One day, you and I will be bowing down before this same throne. Either we will do it willingly in "rejoicing with trembling," or unwillingly in absolute fear and terror, for Scripture clearly says,

> ...So that at the name of Jesus every knee will bow, of those who are in heaven and on earth and under the earth, and that every tongue will confess that Jesus Christ is Lord, to the glory of God the Father. (Philippians 2:10-11)

Which shall it be? As for me, I prefer to fall on my face before Him now with genuine fear and trembling, proclaiming Him as Lord, Savior, King, and The Almighty!

Applying this Lesson:

1. What does "surrender" mean to you?

2. Are you a bondslave like Paul, or does that word offend you? List some verses that describe a bondslave or bondservant.

3. Can you think of another instance when there is a falling, a twisting, and a bowing before the Almighty? Hint: Check out 2 Corinthians 7:15. Write it down below and explain what it means to you.

Lesson 3

"You Wait Only Upon Me–Nothing and No One Else"

We wait for many things in our lives–for the right job, for the right spouse, for the big event to arrive, for things to get better, for someone to show up and make everything right. Sometimes, we wait in anticipation or with great expectation, and sometimes we wait with fear or dread. Most of us are anxiously waiting for something disastrous, troubling, exciting, etc., so much so that the waiting and anticipation control our lives. We go from one anxious event to another and live in a state of slow decay due to fear.

Well, God had something to say about that through King David:

My soul waits in silence for God only; from Him is my salvation. ... My soul, wait in silence for God only, for my hope is from Him. (Psalm 62:1, 5)

What if, instead of waiting for that dreaded phone call, text, or email, we only wait on God? What if we command our soul to wait on God, knowing that He alone is our salvation in every instance and every situation? What if we are so taken up with our fear of the Living God that our first response is to wait on Him in utter silence?

Would waiting change anything?

So what do we do while we are waiting? How many of us lie awake in bed at night worrying about an event that is to happen the next day or even the next week? How many of us endure sleepless nights due to our anxious thoughts? Should we worry while we wait? To that, King David also says:

> *Tremble, and do not sin; meditate in your heart upon your bed, and be still. Offer the sacrifices of righteousness, and trust in the Lord. (Psalm 4:4-5)*

Imagine trembling before the presence of God, and because we are no longer preoccupied with ourselves, we are meditating, literally speaking out loud upon our beds the mighty acts of God, focusing on Him, and being still and in awe before Him. In that way, we offer a real sacrifice of righteousness and genuine trust in the Lord.

Do you think this might eliminate all other fears? I believe it will. How do I know? I have experienced it myself. I take a certain Scripture passage I have memorized, and I whisper it to myself as I am falling asleep. When I do this, my mind stops racing, and I begin to concentrate on the Word of God. While the Word is on my lips, I fall asleep in peace and safety.

David also experienced this, just read the last line of Psalm 4, verse 8:

> *In peace I will both lie down and sleep, for You alone, O Lord, make me to dwell in safety. (Psalm 4:8)*

Now, let's take this idea of waiting only on God and resting in Him a step forward. Let's investigate to see if the Lord Himself said anything concerning this. In Matthew, the Scripture says:

> *Come to Me, all who are weary and heavy-laden, and I will give you rest. (Matthew 11:28)*

Jesus' very first words here are, "*Come to Me.*" These words are specific and exclusive. Do not go to anyone else first, such as doctors, lawyers, psychologists, your best friend, your pastor, or your spouse. No, Jesus tells us, "Come to Me." This is a command. We must not sit in our own anxiety, worry, or depression; we have to "come" to Him. This is very similar to waiting only upon God.

The word "weary" is from the Greek word "kopes" or "kopto" and can mean a reduction of strength due to trouble, lament, and toil. A literal meaning is "to beat the breast in grief." The word for "heavy-laden" is "phortizo" and means "to overburden with ceremony or spiritual anxiety." It could mean to load up with anxiety.

Based on these definitions, Jesus could be speaking directly to you and me in this moment, as we have become overburdened to the point that we are stumbling and breaking under our heavy load of anxiety and worry. And what will He do when we come to Him? He will give us rest.

The word "rest" here comes from the Greek word "anapau," which is made up of two words, "ana" and "pauo." It means to "cease and desist and come to an end with intensity." The kind of rest He gives brings an immediate end to labor, worry, and anxiety, bringing it all to a close–to its final resting place, if you will. I picture myself taking a deep breath and falling back into His arms with a smile on my face, knowing that the burden has now been transferred to the only One who can do something about it.

Verse 29 of Matthew 11 reveals more of what He wants us to do with things that would burden us. Jesus says:

Take my yoke upon you and learn from me. (Matthew 11:29)

Most of us think of a yoke made for oxen when we read this, but that is not the picture that a Jewish rabbi at the time would have. To them (and I think to Jesus), this is the yoke of discipleship, when the disciple becomes so closely linked to the rabbi that they become one.

To "learn" is the Greek term "manthano," meaning to "learn, understand, to know, to be informed, to comprehend, to learn by example." What we're learning here is meekness and a lowly heart; that is, a total dependence on the One we are yoked to, as well as a complete oneness and unity with Him.

Now we come full circle, for when we return to our original theme, "You wait only upon Me, nothing and no one else," we begin to see that Jesus was saying the same thing Himself in Matthew and through King David in the Psalms. To "wait" in the Hebrew language (taken from Psalm 62:1) was a picture of many strands of horsehair being woven together into one strong rope. This takes many hours and even days, much like the idea of waiting and becoming one with God.

When we "come" and are "yoked to" or "woven together" with Jesus, we are becoming one with God.

Waiting only on God is not a metaphor, but an action we must take. Trembling before God, waiting on Him, and meditating on His Word are the only ways we can get rid of our anxious thoughts and truly fear the Lord.

Applying this Lesson:

1. If you haven't already "come" to Jesus and rested from striving and laboring to be something you can never be, take a moment now to lay everything else aside and rest in His presence.

2. Let's take His yoke, follow Him everywhere, read His Word, and know Him so well that we talk with Him all the time. We

may even begin to smell and sound like Him (2 Corinthians 2:14). How do you do this? Well, do you talk to yourself while you are driving to work or the store? Instead, why don't you intentionally ask Jesus a question and see what He says? Have a conversation with Him by asking Him a question like: "What do you think about this, Jesus?" or "What do you see in this person that I am not seeing?"

3. Practice waiting on God by just sitting or walking, getting quiet, and listening for Him to speak. He might surprise you and tell you something you didn't know.

4. You may already be memorizing verses and saying them to yourself, or even using them in evangelism. Let me challenge you to memorize larger sections of Scripture, even chapters; this can change your life! You may even find yourself saying them out loud and finding a new way of waiting on the Lord.

Lesson 4

"You Give Up to Me Your Most Precious Possession"

In Genesis 22, Abraham does not question God, shout at God, or run the other way when God asks this of him:

> *Take now your son, your only son, whom you love, Isaac, and go to the land of Moriah, and offer him there as a burnt offering on one of the mountains of which I will tell you. (Genesis 22:2)*

Personally, I have questioned, shouted, and run away when God has asked me to do something a lot less than what He asked of Abraham—maybe you have, too. These reactions just demonstrate that you and I are human, and He is God.

In Genesis 21, and for the first time in Scripture, Abraham "called on the name of the Lord," and he called Him something specific: "*the Everlasting God.*" This is the first time this name for God is mentioned in Scripture. In Hebrew, Everlasting God can mean the God who cannot die. Some other possible meanings are the God of resurrection and the God who lives forever. The name indicates a deep understanding of the nature, power, and eternal being of God Himself.

When Abraham was asked to sacrifice his son, why didn't he question God? Hebrews 11:19 could reveal a reason:

Reckoning that God was able to raise from the dead, hence he (Abraham) received him back as a type.

Type is referring to a "type" of Jesus, as in Melchizedek in Genesis 14:18 and the serpent on the pole as a type in Numbers 21:9 and John 3:14. With this as a backdrop, we see why Abraham did not question what God asked of him. He knew the eternal and infinite being of God, who has the power to raise the dead; why would he question Him?

We do know, however, it was a "test," since Genesis said earlier:

Now it came about after these things, that God tested Abraham. (Genesis 22:1)

This lesson addresses Abraham's test. It is the same test you and I will face or have already faced (and maybe failed several times): Do you fear God? Will you give up your most precious possession to Him?

Notice this phrase in Genesis 22:2, and again in Genesis 22:12: "*your son, your only son.*" This is very important because God knew it would set up and prepare us for this statement in John 3:16:

For God so loved the world, that He gave His only begotten Son.

God Himself gave up His most precious possession, His only Son, demonstrating a love that surpasses all human comprehension.

Jesus later says this in the Gospel of John to demonstrate what it means to give up your most precious possession:

Truly, Truly (or more literally: Amen, Amen), I say to you, unless a grain of wheat falls into the earth and dies, it remains alone; but if it dies, it bears much fruit. He who loves his life loses it, and he who hates his life in this world will keep it to life eternal. (John 12:24-25)

According to Genesis 22, Abraham was willing to sacrifice Isaac on the altar unto God. Isaac was his one and only son, the only pure seed of the coming Messiah–and in a very real sense, he was Abraham's very life, the most precious thing to him. At the very last minute, while the knife was in the air, God stopped Abraham and provided a ram as a sacrifice instead. Then God said this:

> Do not stretch out your hand against the lad, and do nothing to him; for now I know that you fear God, since you have not withheld your son, your only son, from Me. (Genesis 22:12)

"For now I know that you fear God."

Will you agree with me that to fear God is to love Him above all else, to give up all for Him and to Him? This truth has personally opened my eyes, and I realized that I had yet to give up that one thing I had withheld from Him: my son. I had to release him totally and without hesitation unto God as a sacrifice. Then, I had to trust the God I fear and love to do with my son as He pleased. This meant a change in my prayer life and a change in my attitude towards my son. My prayers are now not focused on what I wanted for my son but on what God had for him (which is far greater, even miraculous). It also meant that instead of having to give my opinion when my son speaks, I would just listen and seek to understand.

How about you? What is that one thing, that one person, or perhaps something about yourself that you are holding back from God? Do you want the truth about why you're holding onto it? It's because whatever it is you are keeping to yourself is more precious to you than God.

Let it go. Give it to Him. Truly fear Him and love Him. Consider Abraham as an example: he did truly fear God by totally obeying him, but at the same time, he loved Him by recognizing that his son Issac actually belonged to God and not to him.

Paul, in his letter to the Galatians, said it this way:

I have been crucified with Christ; and it is no longer I who live, but Christ lives in me; and the life which I now live in the flesh I live by faith in the Son of God, who loved me and gave Himself up for me. (Galatians 2:20)

Applying this Lesson:

1. Meditate on the name "*Everlasting God.*" What does that name mean, and how can it change our understanding of the person of God?

2. In our minds, let's go to Mount Moriah and ask God who or what our most precious possession is. (It may be ourselves.)

3. Let that "grain of wheat" fall to the earth and die (John 12:24). When you let that grain of wheat die, what happens? It forms a seed and sprouts forth with new life. Your grain of wheat may be that dream job; let it die. God has something far better in mind. Consider this verse, apply it to your life and how it changes your relationships to people, events and things:

   I have been crucified with Christ; and it is no longer I who live, but Christ lives in me; and the life which I now live in the flesh I live by faith in the Son of God, who loved me and gave Himself up for me. (Galatians 2:20)

4. Who in Scripture failed the test to give up their most precious possession?

5. Who or what have you lost in the past that still causes you to ask God "why?" Speak it out, yield it to God, and make it a sweet-smelling sacrifice unto Him. (2 Corinthians 2:14-15)

Lesson 5

"You Approach Me with a Broken and Contrite Heart"

How we approach God says a lot about our relationship with Him. It is not only the words we use, but also our attitude, manner, and state of mind. Most of us, knowingly or unknowingly, are full of ourselves and have a false sense of importance. Our culture is full of self-importance, self-acceptance, self-improvement, and self-advancement. This selfish nature is exposed when we approach the Almighty.

Sometimes, we even think our good works will give us a good standing before God. We often come before Him with a sacrifice of some kind. For me, if I am completely honest, that sacrifice is my time. In the back of my mind, I think I am sacrificing my time to come before God and seek Him. You may sense that you are sacrificing something else. But whatever it is, it is probably not a sacrifice. A sacrifice is when we give something up with unreserved abandon. When I give up fifteen minutes of my day to seek the God of Heaven and Earth, that is nothing.

King David, a man after God's own heart, learned the hard way–perhaps the hardest way–through the loss of a child. Through that loss, he realized that he had nothing of value in himself to bring before God to appease the Almighty. Caught in his sin of action and thought, he finally came to this conclusion:

> *For You do not delight in sacrifice, otherwise I would give it; You are not pleased with burnt offering. The sacrifices of God are a broken spirit; a broken and a contrite heart, O God, You will not despise. (Psalm 51:16-17)*

Here is something we cannot work up, dream up, or fake: *a broken heart before God.* That is it, and that is all. A broken heart is the only acceptable posture and the only acceptable sacrifice before God.

The apostle Paul said this:

> *Therefore I urge you, brethren, by the mercies of God, to present your bodies a living and holy sacrifice, acceptable to God which is your spiritual service of worship. (Romans 12:1)*

I am sure you noticed the word "therefore," which always means that the writer is responding to something else. So why is he urging us to offer ourselves as sacrifices? Let's look back a few verses to Romans 11:32:

> *For God has shut up all in disobedience that He may show mercy to all.*

There it is: *the broken and contrite heart "shut up" in our disobedience.* That means there is no way out, and there are no excuses. "Oh, but I really meant to say this, or to do that...." No. You and I are shut up in our own disobedience, which is then why Paul says, "by the mercies of God" (Romans 12:1). This is the only way we can come to God and be a sacrifice to Him—we must recognize that we are shut up in our own disobedience.

King David has one more lesson for us in Psalm 34:9-18. You can read the whole section, but what I want to point out is this:

Come, you children, listen to me; I will teach you the fear of the Lord. (Psalm 34:11)

Wouldn't your ears perk up if you heard this in your prayer time? In context, this is before David is crowned King. He is on the run from Saul, hiding out with his enemy, King Abimelech, and feigning madness. And in the middle of all that is going on, God speaks to David as he is writing this Psalm, ending in this way:

The eyes of the Lord are toward the righteous, and His ears are open to their cry. The face of the Lord is against evildoers, to cut off the memory of them from the earth. The righteous cry and the Lord hears and delivers them out of all their troubles. The Lord is near to the brokenhearted and saves those who are crushed in spirit. (Psalm 34:15-18)

Can you hear and see the theme of the broken, crushed, contrite heart and spirit in these verses? This position of the heart causes the very eyes of God to be upon us and His ears to be open to our cry.

Let's take a deep dive into the Hebrew words for "broken" and "contrite." The Hebrew word for broken is "shabar." It is a prime root and means to break, break down, break off, or break in pieces, and it applies to being brokenhearted as well. It also means to "... crush, destroy, hurt, quench, and tear." Notice the use of "broken" in these verses:

Reproach has broken my heart, and I am so sick. And I looked for sympathy, but there was none, and for comforters, but I found none. They also gave me gall for my food, and for my thirst they gave me vinegar to drink. (Psalm 69:20-21)

For my people have committed two evils: they have forsaken Me, the fountain of living waters, to hew for themselves cisterns, broken cisterns, that can hold no water. (Jeremiah 2:13)

He heals the brokenhearted and binds up their wounds. (Psalm 147:3)

The Hebrew word for contrite is "dakah." It means to crumble, to bruise, to crush into powder, or to collapse. A very close cousin, "dakkah" means to mutilate or wound. We can see the theme of "dakah" or "dakkah" through these verses:

> *For thus says the high and exalted One who lives forever, whose name is Holy, "I dwell on a high and holy place, and also with the contrite and lowly of spirit in order to revive the spirit of the lowly and to revive the heart of the contrite." (Isaiah 57:15)*

> *"For my hand made all these things, thus all these things came into being," declares the Lord. "But to this one I will look, to him who is humble and contrite of spirit, and who trembles at My Word." (Isaiah 66:2)*

The verse from Psalm 69 especially hits me hard. This is, without a doubt, a prophecy concerning the brokenness of Jesus of Nazareth. The Scripture provides a moment to contemplate the "reproach" that came from the Father when all the sin of the world was piled onto Jesus. Jesus' heart was "shabar." It was crushed, destroyed, torn apart, and broken into pieces. This reproach and separation from God the Father had to have been more painful than the physical pain. And yet, this crushing of Jesus is the only sacrifice that is acceptable to God: Jesus is the broken and contrite heart we need. I am looking at this differently now because neither you nor I can be broken in the same way that Jesus Christ was broken, so it has to be His substitute of brokenness that God accepts. It is that substitute–the acceptance of what Jesus did– that you and I must offer in complete fear and humility in order to be forgiven, redeemed, and made whole.

What is your attitude when you approach God with your most heartfelt, heartrending request? Do you want to appeal to His deep, never-ending mercies, and come brokenhearted and contrite before Him?

Applying this Lesson:

1. Read Psalm 34 and note each time you see the word "fear." Then, go back and read the context. What is God trying to tell you personally?

2. Read Psalm 69 and underline each mention of the word "reproach." Note the context and write out what you learned. Have you fully received your wholeness for Christ's brokenness? Read 1 Corinthians 11:23-26, KJV:

For I have received of the Lord that which also I delivered unto you. That the Lord Jesus, the same night in which he was betrayed, took bread: and when he had given thanks, he brake it, and said, Take, eat: this is my body, which is broken for you: this do in remembrance of me. After the same manner also he took the cup, when he had supped, saying, this cup is the new testament in my blood: this do ye as oft as ye drink it, in remembrance of me.

Lesson 6

"When You Truly Fear Me, You Need Not Fear Anything or Anyone Else"

Fear has a way of consuming us, haunting us, and taking over our thoughts—sometimes even our lives. Chances are, you have heard the phrase "paralyzed by fear," or perhaps you have even experienced it. Sometimes, our fear is well-founded. But most of the time, that anxious thought that turns into fear never becomes reality, and we waste days, if not weeks, imagining that which never happens—all due to fear.

Let's step back a minute, though. What if that fear was placed on the One who deserves it, and instead of bringing the most dreadful outcome upon us, He brings the best outcome? Oh, and then that fear of God will banish all other fears?

Yes, a true fear of God delivers us from all other fears. Take Psalm 112, for example. Verse 1 says this:

Praise the Lord! How blessed is the man who fears the LORD, who greatly delights in His commandments.

If you skip down a few verses, you will find this:

He will not fear evil tidings; his heart is steadfast, trusting in the LORD. His heart is upheld, he will not fear, until he looks with satisfaction on his adversaries. (Psalm 112:7-8)

Here is the key to our problem of fearing the "what ifs" of life: once we truly fear God and delight in His Word, we become blessed. Blessed is the Hebrew word "esher", and it means "happy" or "happiness." The word also appears in Psalm 65:4 "Blessed is the man whom thou choosest," and in Psalm 84:4, "Blessed are they that dwell in thy house." But we not only gain a certain happiness when we fear the Lord, we will also no longer fear any evil tidings. It does not matter where those evil tidings come from–a person, a thing, or a thought or whisper from the evil one–we will not fear them. Why? Because we are so focused on God and His Word that our "heart is steadfast" and our "heart is upheld." In Hebrew, "His heart is upheld" translates into "confident in Jehovah is held his heart." Our confidence, produced by that Godly fear and delight, is so completely focused on Jehovah that now He is the one who is holding and guarding our hearts.

This leads us perfectly to Psalm 27:

The Lord is my light and my salvation; whom shall I fear? The Lord is the defense of my life; whom shall I dread? When evildoers came upon me to devour my flesh, my adversaries and my enemies, they stumbled and fell, though a host encamp against me, my heart will not fear, though war arise against me, in spite of this I shall be confident. (Psalm 27:1-3)

I think these verses cover everything and everyone, including evildoers, adversaries, enemies, and even a host surrounding us. We do not have to fear anything or anyone when we fear the Lord.

Do you remember Elisha and his servant in 2 Kings 6:8-17? His servant woke up one morning and saw the entire army of Aram surrounding the place where he and Elisha were sleeping. He panicked and asked Elisha, "What shall we do?" Elisha said only two things: 1) "Do not fear, for those who are with us are more than those who are with them," and 2) "O, LORD, open his eyes that he may see." Do you know what happened next? God did open his eyes (the eyes of his heart) and saw myriads of angelic beings with horses and chariots of fire surrounding Aram's army. May God open our eyes to see with the eyes of our heart, to see what He sees.

Paul's eyes had been opened. Here is what he said in his letter to the Romans:

> For I am persuaded, (another translation says, "convinced"), that neither death, nor life, nor angels, nor principalities, nor things present, nor things to come, nor powers, nor height, nor depth, nor any other created thing, will be able to separate us from the love of God, which is in Christ Jesus our Lord. (Romans 8:38-39)

Where is our excuse to worry, be anxious, and fear? I think we just lost it somewhere in between "delight," "confident," and "blessed" (Psalm 112:1 and Romans 8:38, see above).

And if that isn't enough, here is the final evidence for fearing the Lord and not man: Psalm 118.

Oh, let those who fear the LORD say, "His Mercy is everlasting." (Psalm 118:4) (Another translation says, "His Lovingkindness is Everlasting." Either way, it is a covenant term, meaning God is in covenant with us to keep all His promises.)

> From my distress I called upon the Lord; the Lord answered me and set me in a large place. The Lord is for me; I will not fear; what can man do to me? The Lord is for me among those who help me. (Psalm 118:57)

These words are exactly what the Levites sang as the Israelites went into battle against Moab and Ammon, their most aggressive enemies:

> Give thanks to the Lord, for His Lovingkindness is everlasting. (2 Chronicles 20:21)

The Levites, marching in front of the army, sang this over and over again, and their enemies were routed and defeated. (You can read the whole glorious story in 2 Chronicles 20.)

Let's believe all of our enemies are routed and destroyed, fear only our God, delight in His Word, and sing to the top of our lungs, "Give thanks to the Lord, for His lovingkindness is everlasting!" And let's not forget what Jesus said in John 14:1:

> *Do not let your heart be troubled; believe in God, believe also in Me.*

Applying this Lesson:

1. Pick one of these verses to memorize: Psalm 112:1, 7-8; Psalm 27:1-3; Psalm 119:23-24; Proverbs 19:23; Isaiah 41:10.

2. When anxiety raises its ugly head (and it will), speak these verses in the question above out loud and start believing them.

3. How do we convince ourselves that what God said is true and all our fears are unfounded? Let's start with the first premise, that nearly everything we think of ourselves is false. Once we accept that, then we can begin to believe that everything in Scripture is true, which is the second premise. Now, we can begin to quote to ourselves what is true–Scripture. The more we speak the truth of the Scripture to ourselves, the more we believe it. Soon we are convinced and can say with Paul:

> *I am convinced (or fully persuaded) that neither death, nor life, nor angels, nor principalities, nor things present, nor things to come, nor powers, nor height, nor depth, nor any other created thing, shall be able to separate me from the love of God which is in Christ Jesus. (Romans 8:38-39)*

Lesson 7

"When You Truly Fear Me, It Brings the Highest Form of Revelation"

Revelation is a very interesting subject on its own, as there are many kinds of revelation, many of which can be very subjective. For instance, a revelation can come in the form of a dream, a vision, or a thought while you are driving or hiking down a trail. My greatest revelations come as I meditate on a section of Scripture, ask God questions, and then wait for His answer. The entire Word of God is a revelation and should be treated as such.

In this lesson, we are going to look at several revelations and prophecies in the Word of God. You have to have a revelation to prophecy, so they are closely related. The prophecy in its most simplistic form is a telling forth. Which means you can have a revelation without prophesying. Now, let's investigate what happened before the revelation and whether there was a fear of God involved.

Isaiah Chapters 1 through 5 give a full picture of the historical basis of what had happened in Israel before Isaiah had the following revelation of God. As God, through Isaiah's revelation, listed the offenses of Israel and Judah, He used phrases like, "but they have revolted against Me" and "the whole head is sick." He compares them with Sodom and Gomorrah and then says this:

> What are your multiplied sacrifices to Me?" says the Lord. "I have had enough of burnt offerings of rams and the fat of fed cattle; and I take no pleasure in the blood of bulls, lambs or goats. (Isaiah 1:11)

Sound familiar? It's a lot like Psalm 51:17, where these sacrifices again were no longer acceptable. But what was acceptable? From Lesson 6, we learned that a sacrifice leading to a broken and contrite heart, which is Jesus, is the only acceptable sacrifice.

Isaiah continues to prophesy in Chapter 2:

> The proud look of man will be abased, and the loftiness of man will be humbled, and the Lord alone will be exalted in that day. For the Lord of hosts will have a day of reckoning against everyone who is proud and lofty and against everyone who is lifted up, that he may be abased. ... Men will go into caves and rocks and into holes in the ground before the terror of the LORD and the splendor of His majesty, when He arises to make the earth tremble. (Isaiah 2:11-12, 19)

After Isaiah declares the six woes, which are specific judgments from God for specific sins, Isaiah continues his prophecy with this:

> Therefore, as a tongue of fire consumes stubble and dry grass collapses into the flame, so their root will become like rot and their blossom blow away as dust; for they have rejected the law of the Lord of hosts and despised the word of the Holy One of Israel. On this account the anger of the Lord has burned against His people, and He has stretched out His hand against them and struck them down. And the mountains quaked, and their corpses lay like refuse in the middle of the streets. For all this His anger is not spent, but His hand is still stretched out. (Isaiah 5:24-25)

This is the setting for Chapter 6, Isaiah's vision, and the Fear of the Lord was very prevalent and perhaps even overwhelming, so much so that Isaiah declared the seventh woe upon himself.

In the year of King Uzziah's death, I saw the Lord sitting on a throne, lofty and exalted, with the train of His robe filling the temple. Seraphim stood above Him, each having six wings: with two he covered his face, and with two he covered his feet, and with two he flew. And one called out to another and said, "Holy, Holy, Holy, is the Lord of hosts, the whole earth is full of His glory." And the foundations of the thresholds trembled at the voice of him who called out, while the temple was filling with smoke. Then I said, "Woe is me, for I am ruined! Because I am a man of unclean lips, and I live among a people of unclean lips; for my eyes have seen the King, the Lord of hosts." (Isaiah 6:1)

This vision of the throne room of God is exceptional. There were only three visions of the throne room of God in Scripture that I know of: The vision in the book of Job, the vision in the book of Revelation, and Isaiah's vision that we are reading about here. Even then, there were no details in the other visions of the robe, the smoke, and the thresholds trembling. This vision, caused by great trembling, fear, and the death of the king, became even more pronounced with Isaiah's response, "Woe is me, for I am ruined!"

This was the correct response, and the only response when we are in the presence of the Almighty. For Isaiah knew that he was undone, ruined, without excuse, and headed for judgment unless God extended His Mercy. It was at that moment when the Seraphim touched his lips with the hot coal and cleansed his sin so Isaiah could hear the voice of the Lord saying,

Whom shall I send and who will go for Us? (Isaiah 6:8)

Lucius Malcolm

It appears that Isaiah's revelation and vision of God and His throne were directly related to the fear of God. In His presence, the earth trembles, and smoke fills the temple.

Daniel was a prophet in his own right, having the gift of dreams and the gift of interpretation. His book is filled with amazing revelation of God's ways and character, as well as prophetic words concerning the death of Christ and His return. If you have not done a study on this amazing book, I encourage you to do so. For this lesson concerning the fear of God, we will look at a few of Daniel's visions, starting in Chapter 10.

> *I lifted up my eyes and looked, and behold, there was a certain man dressed in linen, whose waist was girded with a belt of pure gold of Uphaz. His body also was like beryl, his face had the appearance of lightning, his eyes were like flaming torches, his arms and feet like the gleam of polished bronze, and the sound of his words like the sound of a tumult. (Daniel 10:5-6)*

Daniel's response was this:

> *Now I, Daniel, alone saw the vision, while the men who were with me did not see the vision; nevertheless, a great dread fell on them, and they ran away to hide themselves. So I was left alone and saw this great vision; yet no strength was left in me for my natural color turned to a deathly pallor, and I retained no strength. But I heard the sound of His words; and as soon as I heard the sound of His words, I fell into a deep sleep on my face, with my face to the ground. (Daniel 10:7-9)*

Prior to this vision, Daniel was in mourning for three weeks and fasted from "tasty" food, meat, and wine (Daniel 1:12). I do not know if you have ever fasted before. There are many examples of fasting in the Bible, the most famous being Jesus himself, who appeared to have fasted in preparation for the temptation that was coming (Matthew 4:1-2). Daniel fasted to have a clearer vision of what God wanted to say to him. Another good reason to fast is for direction and for when we are floundering in life. The fast will clear our minds, making us more aware of God's presence and more sensitive to His Word and thereby bring a clear understanding of God's love, His greatness and His Holiness. Fasting will produce the kind of fear and awe that produces revelation.

Through Daniel's fast, we can learn the correct preparation for a revelation and vision of this nature. But beware: along with the fasting and the revelation can come dread, a lack of strength, total weakness, and a falling on our face.

Consider this vision:

> *And behold, one who resembled a human being was touching my lips; then I opened my mouth and spoke and said to him who was standing before me, "O my lord, as a result of the vision, anguish has come upon me and I have retained no strength. For how can such a servant of my lord talk with such as my lord? As for me, there remains just now no strength in me, nor has any breath been left in me." (Daniel 10:16)*

It is now evident that fearing God brings the highest form of revelation. Scripture has proven this. However, this lesson would be incomplete without mentioning John in his book of Revelation:

> *When I saw Him, I fell at His feet like a dead man. And He placed His right hand upon me saying, "Do not be afraid; I am the first and the last." (Revelation 1:17)*

John's revelations had begun, and he was about to receive the revelation of all revelations. His first response? Great fear to the point of being like a dead man.

Out of Psalm 25, we have King David summing up this whole lesson for us when he says:

The secret of the Lord is for those who fear Him, and He will make them know (or reveal) His covenant. (Psalm 25:14)

"Secret" can be translated as "intimate moments," and the revelation of His covenant is the understanding of all of Scripture from the covenant of Adam to the covenant with Jesus. With this in mind, who does not want to fear the Lord and receive His revelation?

Applying this Lesson:

1. Ask yourself: do you really want deeper and greater revelation? Or are you happy with just going to church, hearing a sermon, and singing songs?

2. Prepare yourself with fasting, mourning (blessed are they that mourn), and long periods of being alone with God (Matthew 5:3-4). I suggest you commit to a time and place to sit with God. Be sure and alert your family to your plans, so they will understand. Then get still and begin to listen. This will take practice–the revelation will not happen overnight, and the proper fear of God is the beginning.

3. Being intimately acquainted with the written Word of God is one of the most important keys to revelation. Since Jesus is the Word, the written and the spoken word, it makes sense to know it. So, I recommend reading it, then read it again–it is inexhaustible. If you need a place to start, start with the Gospel according to John.

4. The Lord God is still asking this same question today that He asked throughout the Bible, *"Whom shall I send and who will go for Us? (Isaiah 6:8a)."* Have you heard Him call your name and say this to you? Perhaps it is your turn to say, *"Here I am, send me (Isaiah 6:8b)."*

Lesson 8

"When You Fear Me, A New Hope Arises in Your Soul, Knowing that the Victory Is Certain"

Some commentators will say that Psalm 96 is the song that the 144,000 sang in Revelation 14, and it does fit. But for now, let us picture ourselves singing this song, blessing His name, proclaiming the good tidings, and telling of His glory and His wonderful deeds to the nations:

> For great is the Lord and greatly to be praised; He is to be feared above all gods. For all the gods of the peoples are idols, but the Lord made the heavens. Splendor and majesty are before Him, strength and beauty are in His sanctuary. Ascribe (this is a Hebrew term meaning to give your all) to the Lord, O families of the peoples, ascribe to the Lord glory and strength.
>
> Ascribe to the Lord the glory of His name; bring an offering and come into His courts (are you still singing?).
>
> Worship the Lord in holy attire (the beauty of holiness); tremble before Him (this is more than the emotion of fear— there is some pain involved, as the trembling leads to falling on one's face), all the earth.
> Say among the nations, "The Lord reigns; indeed the world is firmly established, it will not be moved; He will judge the peoples with equity." (Psalm 96:4-10)

As we end with verse 13, notice how the singing of this Psalm brings the hope and assurance that God, the Lord, is in full control as we tremble before Him and sing of His splendor and majesty:

> *Before the Lord, for He is coming, for He is coming to judge the earth. He will judge the world in righteousness, and the peoples in His faithfulness. (Psalm 96:13)*

Great hope fills my heart in knowing that He is coming (repeated twice) and that He will judge (also repeated twice).

As I said earlier, this Psalm 96 could be the "new song" mentioned in Revelation 14:

> *And I saw another angel flying in midheaven, having an eternal gospel to preach to those who live on the earth, and to every nation and tribe and tongue and people; and he said with a loud voice, "Fear God, and give Him glory, because the hour of His judgment has come; worship Him who made the heaven and the earth and sea and springs of waters." (Revelation 14:6-7)*

Another wonderful Psalm where we see this same hope arise out of fear of the Lord is Psalm 89:

> *The heavens will praise Your wonders, O Lord; Your faithfulness also in the assembly of the holy ones. For who in the skies is comparable to the Lord? Who among the sons of the mighty is like the Lord, a God greatly feared in the council of the holy ones, and awesome (or terrible) above all those who are around Him? (Psalm 89:5-7)*

> *How blessed are the people who know the joyful sound (or shouts of joy)! O, Lord, they walk in the light of Your countenance. (Psalm 89:15)*

We need to ask ourselves: do we know that sound? Why the shouts of joy? Scripture usually answers itself, so just go back a few verses to verse 12 to see what elicited these joyful responses:

The north and the south, You have created them; Tabor and Hermon shout for joy at Your name. (Psalm 89:12)

    Tabor and Hermon were mountains where great victories from the hand of the Lord came to pass, so the shouts of joy are due to the victory. This makes perfect sense when we read, "How blessed are the people who know the joyful sound" (or shouts of joy). Do you know? Can you hear that joyful sound of victory? Start praising Him, trembling before Him, and living in His presence, and you will hear the sound of victory and the shouts of joy.

    Psalm 118:15-16 says this:

The sound of joyful shouting and salvation is in the tents of the righteous; the right hand of the Lord is doing with might (that is what my Hebrew psalter says), the right hand of the Lord is exalted; the right hand of the LORD is doing with might. (Hebrew psalter)

    This is a continuous victory and exaltation of the right hand of God, who is none other than the Lord Jesus Christ, and His victory over sin, death, and hell. Now, compare this to Paul's prayer for us in Ephesians 1 and see how he exalts Jesus Christ and declares victory:

I pray that the eyes of your heart may be enlightened, so that you will know what is the hope of His calling, what are the riches of the glory of His inheritance in the saints, and what is the surpassing greatness of His power toward us who believe. These are in accordance with the working of the strength of His might which He brought about in Christ, when He raised Him from the dead and seated Him at His right hand in the heavenly places, far above all rule and authority and power and dominion, and every name that is named, not only in this age but also in the one to come. And He put all things in subjection under his feet, and gave Him as head over all things to the church. (Ephesians 1:18-22)

That is shouting ground. The right hand of the Lord, Jesus Christ, has won the victory, once and for all. Next time you are feeling defeated and you see no way out, quote Paul, but make it personal:

When you, Oh God, raised the Lord Jesus from the dead, you raised me from the dead, when you seated Him above all rule and authority, you seated me with Him. When you put all things under His feet, you also put them under my feet. I can fear you, my God and live in the victory that you have won through my Lord Jesus Christ!

Then we begin to learn the fear the Lord and start shouting for joy because the battle is over and the victory is won through our Lord Jesus, the ruling King over heaven and earth.

Applying this Lesson:

1. Let's go back to the verses in Psalms 96 and Psalm 89 mentioned above and read, shout, and sing them out loud. We do not do this enough. Singing and reading God's Word out loud helps reinforce the words. We can proclaim His victory over and over.

2. Think about a time when God brought you through a battle and won the victory. Go back and thank God for your Mount Tabor and Mount Hermon experiences.

3. Let's practice hope. Romans 5:2 says, "We exult in hope of the glory of God." This life and its trials and tribulations are not about us and our comfort but about the glory of God. Let's practice rejoicing in genuine hope–that is, the idea that God will get glory out of this situation no matter what. Here's an example:

   Lord, I do not like the fact that my daughter has just overdosed on drugs, but I am going to praise You anyway, because You are the God of miracles and will take this tragedy and turn it to her good by drawing her to You, and You will bring yourself glory by teaching me how to trust you more. I am going to speak healing and restoration in the name of Jesus over her right now. The brother of Jesus, James, said it this way, "Count it all joy, my brethren, when you encounter various trials….."(James 1:2)

Lesson 9

"When You Fear Me, You Delight in My Word, and Blessings Follow"

This lesson brings focus to what is shown throughout the Bible--the truth that when we can delight in God's Word, blessings will follow. From Abraham and Moses to David and Solomon, and of course, the Lord Jesus, we see this truth acted out over and over again. Solomon said in Ecclesiastes 8:12:

> Although a sinner does evil a hundred times and may lengthen his life, still I know that it will be well for those who fear God, who fear Him openly.

Ecclesiastes 8:12 is written this way in the Jubilee Bible 2000:

> Though a sinner does evil one hundred times and his judgment is prolonged, yet surely I know that it shall be well with those that fear God, who fear before his presence.

"It shall be well" means God's blessings on those who fear Him.

Psalm 112, most likely written by David, instructs and proclaims:

> *Praise the Lord! How blessed is the man who fears the Lord, who greatly delights in His commandments. His descendants will be mighty on earth; the generation of the upright will be blessed. Wealth and riches are in his house, and his righteousness endures forever. Light arises in the darkness for the upright; he is gracious and compassionate and righteous. It is well with the man who is gracious and lends; he will maintain his cause in judgment. For he will never be shaken; the righteous will be remembered forever. He will not fear evil tidings; his heart is steadfast, trusting in the Lord. His heart is upheld, he will not fear, until he looks with satisfaction on his adversaries. He has given freely to the poor, his righteousness endures forever; his horn will be exalted in honor. The wicked will see it and be vexed, he will gnash his teeth and melt away; the desire of the wicked will perish.*

I know this is a lengthy Scripture, but bear with me. Notice the beginning of the Psalm: "How blessed is the man who fears the Lord, who greatly delights in His commandments." This statement is the reason for all the blessings and favor from God that follow: the man fears the Lord and delights in His Word.

I have held on to this Psalm ever since I went through a terrible time of loneliness, desertion, and betrayal, when my former wife left me with a newborn and a two-year-old. I have realized some of the blessings listed within the Psalm as I applied fearing the Lord and delighting in His Word. Here are a few:

> *Wealth and Riches in His house (vs 3) This happened over a long period as I learned that the Lord owned everything, and the more I gave it away, the more He brought riches and true wealth to me.*

> *The righteousness of Christ enduring forever (vs 3). This happened as I recognized the truth of Romans 6, that the very righteousness of Christ was imputed to me and I no longer had to earn it.*

Light arising when all was dark because I focused on Him (vs 4) This came about in the dark hours of the night when I was exhausted in caring for 2 small children on my own and ready to give up. As I gave up, Jesus came to me in the night and gave me the power to look at Him and not the loneliness and heartache.

Not fearing evil tidings, because God Himself held my heart and caused me to look with satisfaction upon my adversaries (vs 7-8) This has happened over and over as thoughts and evil events would scare me until I would realize that God himself was holding my heart and giving me courage to face another day.

Do you see how this works?

Psalm 1 begins by describing one who fears the Lord and delights in His law:

How blessed is the man who does not walk in the counsel of the wicked, nor stand in the path of sinners, nor sit in the seat of scoffers! But his delight is in the law of the Lord, and in His law he meditates day and night. He will be like a tree firmly planted by streams of water, which yields its fruit in its season and its leaf does not wither; and in whatever he does, he prospers. (Psalm 1:1-3)

There is a definite connection between the fear of the Lord, delighting in God's Word, and the blessings of God. The Lord Jesus puts it this way:

But seek first the kingdom of God and his righteousness, and all these things will be added to you. (Matthew 6:33, ESV)

What are "all these things"? All the things we are anxious about on a daily basis: what we will eat, what we will wear, what tomorrow will bring, where the money will come from? But we are to seek what first? His kingdom, His righteousness.

When we do this, we fear Him above all else. Is it not like the Son of God to put it so simply and yet communicate with such power? I would also point out this quote from Him:

> *If you abide in Me, and My words abide in you, ask whatever you wish, and it will be done for you. (John 15:7)*

Let's look at the similarity of these statements: "abide in Me," "fear the Lord," "seek first," and "greatly delights." I see a clear message communicated in different ways—with Jesus, of course, pulling it all together.

As I am abiding in Him and allowing His words to abide in me, I am fearing Him above all others and exalting His word above all else. This is when He begins to add "all these things." In Psalm 112, we see some of these "things" that God is promising: my descendants are mighty on the earth, my generation is blessed, wealth and riches are in my house, my righteousness endures forever, light arises in the darkness for me, I become gracious and compassionate, I will never be shaken, I will not fear evil tidings, and my heart is steadfast, trusting in the Lord.

I hope you can see how this works. It is so simple, yet so difficult for our flesh. If I were completely meditating on God's word day and night and fully abiding in Him, every request from my lips would be answered, and all that I did would prosper. However, that is just not the case. Even Paul said:

> *For we know that the Law is spiritual, but I am of flesh, sold into bondage to sin. For what I am doing, I do not understand; for I am not practicing what I would like to do, but I am doing the very thing I hate. (Romans 7:14-15)*

We are in a constant battle, my brothers and sisters, and yet the truth of my original statement still stands: the one who fears the Lord will delight in His Word, and blessings will follow. As for he who seeks the kingdom of God first, all these things will be added unto him.

But what if we could take it a step further? Paul says this in his letter to the Ephesians:

Blessed be the God and Father of our Lord Jesus Christ, who has blessed us with every spiritual blessing in the heavenly places in Christ. (Ephesians 1:13)

Alright then, are you and I in Christ? Yes. If you believe in Jesus as Lord and Savior, our only means to the Father who is in heaven, then you are in Christ.

Have we received (past tense) every spiritual blessing? Yes.

But, you say, these are spiritual blessings, not real, earthly blessings. And I would say you are right. The word spiritual in Greek means non-carnal, non-human, and supernatural; the meaning comes from the root word, "pneuma," meaning "breath." These blessings are God-breathed: chosen, predestined, adopted, redeemed, holy, blameless, and forgiven (Ephesians 1:4-7). These blessings cannot be taken from us, and they last into eternity. Real blessings.

Therefore, since we already have these blessings, we can begin our walk of faith from a place of very real blessings, which gives us the power and the inclination to abide in Him, to delight in His commandments, to seek Him first, and to fear the Lord with trembling.

As we focus on the one, undeniable blessing of knowing Him, abiding in Him and He in us–we will indeed have all "things" added to us.

Now do you see, with Peter, how *"His divine power has granted to us everything pertaining to life and godliness, through the true knowledge of Him who called us by His own glory and excellence" (2 Peter 1:3)*?

Applying this Lesson:

1. Simply believe Scripture! You and I have it all: all the spiritual blessings, everything about life and godliness (2 Peter 1:3).

2. Now the practical side: Let's speak these promises over ourselves out loud when we rise in the morning, when we fall asleep at night, when we are waiting for the children to arrive home from school, etc. Let's post them on our mirror or put them on 3x5 cards and say them over and over so we never forget them:

   I am a born-again man or woman with a new heart and a renewed mind. (2 Corinthians 5:17)

   I was chosen before the foundation of the world. (Ephesians 1:4)

   I am adopted into the family of God with the right of inheritance. (Romans 8:15-17)

   I am redeemed from our life of sin and death (that is, bought from slavery by the very blood of Christ). (Galatians 4:4-7, 5:1)

   I am Holy and blameless before God, which means there is absolutely nothing that the enemy can use to accuse me. (1 Thessalonians 3:13)

   I challenge you to memorize and meditate on Psalm 112. It changed my life during a very difficult time—it can change yours for the better too!

Lesson 10

"When You Fear Me, My Wisdom Begins"

Today's culture seldom associates wisdom with fear. We might associate it with more education, more degrees, or more experience, or even with getting older. We do get wiser with age, don't we?

Instead, God's wisdom (different from worldly wisdom) is initiated by fear, for it says in Proverbs 9:10, "The fear of the Lord is the beginning of wisdom and the knowledge of the Holy one is understanding." Then God repeats himself through King David in Psalm 111:10; repetition is always an indication of importance.

The word for "beginning" in Proverbs 9:10 is the Hebrew word "techillah," which means "to open" or the very initial start of something (from Strong's Concordance). Picture opening the door and preparing to step into the room of wisdom.

The word for "beginning" in Psalm 111:10 is a little different. It is the Hebrew word "reshiyth," which refers to "first fruit" (also from Strong's Concordance). And so, not only does the fear of the Lord open the door to wisdom, but it is also the water and sunshine that produce that first taste of wisdom in our lives.

So what is wisdom? There are myriads of books written on the subject of wisdom, but Proverbs 8 gives an exhaustive definition. I encourage you to stop and read the entire chapter before you continue.

Now let me point out a few verses in Proverbs 8 and what I believe they reveal:

About WISDOM...	Proverbs
Wisdom calls.	8:1
It utters truth.	8:7
It dwells with prudence, knowledge, and discretion.	8:12
Wisdom is understanding.	8:14
Power belongs to wisdom.	8:14
Kings and princes reign and rule through the power of wisdom.	8:15-16
Wisdom has the capacity to love those who love Him.	8:17
If you seek Him, you will find Him.	8:17
The LORD (Yaweh) possessed wisdom before the earth was established.	8:22
Wisdom was the master workman of creation and marked out the foundation of the earth.	8:29-30
Wisdom has His delight in the sons of men.	8:31

Are you seeing what I am seeing?

Can wisdom be anything or anyone other than Jesus Christ Himself?

Now let's link a few New Testament verses:

John 14:21: "and he who loves me shall be loved by My Father and I will love him" (compare Proverbs 8:17)

Matthew 28:18: "all authority has been given to Me in heaven and on earth" (compare Proverbs 8:15-16)

John 1:3: "All things came into being by Him and apart from Him nothing came into being that has come into being" (compare Proverbs 8:23-29)

Matthew 7:7-8: "Ask and it shall be given to you, Seek and you will find, Knock and the door will be opened to you" (compare Proverbs 8:1)

Matthew 11:28: "Come unto me all who are weary and heavy laden and I will give you rest" (compare Proverbs 8:1)

1 John 2:27: "And as for you, the anointing which you received from Him abides in you, and you have no need for anyone to teach you; but as His anointing teaches you about all things, and is true and is not a lie, and just as it has taught you, abide in Him" (compare Proverbs 8:12)

So now we have connected wisdom with Christ, and to solidify this idea, look at 1 Corinthians 2:24, "But to those who are the called, both Jew and Greeks, Christ, the power of God and The Wisdom of God. And in the same section, 1 Corinthians 1:30: "but by His doing, you are in Christ Jesus, who was made to us wisdom from God" (Interlinear Greek-English translation).

To summarize, if the fear of the Lord is the entryway, the beginning, the portal into the wisdom of God, then we find that very wisdom in Christ. It is imparted to us as we dwell in Him and He in us. And it is that very fear of God that drives us to surrender to Him. This surrender is the portal, or the first step, into wisdom.

Applying this Lesson:

1. How are you doing in the area of true wisdom? Have you fully surrendered to the One who is Wisdom?

2. Is the fear of God in the Old Testament the same as the love of God in the New Testament? Is there a link between the two?

3. When was the last time you actually sought out the wisdom of God?

To conclude this study, I must address this question:

What Happens When You Don't Fear the Lord?

Psalm 36:1-4 (KJV) speaks directly to this:

The transgression of the wicked saith within my heart, that there is no fear of God before his eyes. For he flattereth himself in his own eyes, until his iniquity be found to be hateful. The words of his mouth are iniquity and deceit: he hath left off to be wise, and to do good. He deviseth mischief upon his bed; he setteth himself in a way that is not good; he abhorreth not evil.

Later, Romans says this:

There is none who understands, there is none who seeks for God; all have turned aside, together they have become useless; there is none who does good, there is not even one.

Their throat is an open grave, with their tongues they keep deceiving, the poison of asps is under their lips; whose mouth is full of cursing and bitterness; their feet are swift to shed blood, destruction and misery are in their paths, and the path of peace they have not known.

There is no fear of God before their eyes. (Romans 3:11-18)

There you have it—what a clear differentiation. Either we fear God and surrender to His lordship and authority, and goodness and mercy follow us wherever we go, or we declare ourselves as gods, and destruction and misery follow us wherever we go.

Thank you for taking this journey with me. My prayer and hope is that these lessons have taken you to a new place of fellowship with the Almighty. If you have any questions, please feel free to contact me at luciusj61@gmail.com.

Lucius Malcolm

www.ingramcontent.com/pod-product-compliance
Lightning Source LLC
Chambersburg PA
CBHW060429050426
42449CB00009B/2200